P9-CJH-193

Magic Tricks

TREASURE BAY

Parent's Introduction

Welcome to **We Read Phonics**! This series is designed to help you assist your child in reading. Each book includes a story, as well as some simple word games to play with your child. The games focus on the phonics skills and sight words your child will use in reading the story.

Here are some recommendations for using this book with your child:

1 **Word Play**

There are word games both before and after the story. Make these games fun and playful. If your child becomes bored or frustrated, play a different game or take a break.

Phonics is a method of sounding out words by blending together letter sounds. However, not all words can be "sounded out." **Sight words** are frequently used words that usually cannot be sounded out.

2 Read the Story

After some word play, read the story aloud to your child—or read the story together, by reading aloud at the same time or by taking turns. As you and your child read, move your finger under the words.

Next, have your child read the entire story to you while you follow along with your finger under the words. If there is some difficulty with a word, either help your child to sound it out or wait about five seconds and then say the word.

3 Discuss and Read Again

After reading the story, talk about it with your child. Ask questions like, "What happened in the story?" and "What was the best part?" It will be helpful for your child to read this story to you several times. Another great way for your child to practice is by reading the book to a younger sibling, a pet, or even a stuffed animal!

So what did you like most in this book?

I really liked the trick with the crayon! I'd like to try it!

LEVEL 5
Level 5 introduces words with "ai" and "ay" with the long "a" sound (as in *bait* and *day*), "igh," "y," and "ie" with the long "i" sound (as in *high, cry,* and *tied*), and the "ng" sound (as in *song* and *king*). Also included are the word endings -er and -ing (as in *higher* and *running*).

Magic Tricks

A We Read Phonics™ Book
Level 5

Text Copyright © 2011 by Treasure Bay, Inc.
Illustrations Copyright © 2011 by Meredith Johnson

Reading Consultants: Bruce Johnson, M.Ed., and Dorothy Taguchi, Ph.D.

We Read Phonics™ is a trademark of Treasure Bay, Inc.

Published by
Treasure Bay, Inc.
P.O. Box 119
Novato, CA 94948 USA

Printed in Singapore

Library of Congress Catalog Card Number: 2010932589

Hardcover ISBN: 978-1-60115-337-1
Paperback ISBN: 978-1-60115-338-8

We Read Phonics™
Patent Pending

Visit us online at:
www.TreasureBayBooks.com

PR-11-10

Magic Tricks

By Sindy McKay

Illustrated by Meredith Johnson

Phonics Game

Picture Walk

Help prepare your child to read the story by previewing pictures and words.

1. Turn to page 4. Point to the words *magic* and *tricks.* Ask your child what type of trick the boy might be doing in the picture. Read the sentence to your child.

2. On page 5, read the words "Try to do the tricks in this book." Ask your child if he thinks he could do a trick. Ask your child to point to and say the words *try* and *book.* You might want to point out that the "y" in *try* makes the long "i" sound.

3. Turn to page 6. Read the words "This is what you will need." Ask your child to look at the picture and predict what might be needed for the tricks.

4. Continue "walking" through the story, asking questions about the pictures or the words. Encourage your child to talk about the pictures and words you point out.

5. As you move through the story, you can also help your child read some of the new or more difficult words.

Sight Word Game

Go Fish

Play this game to practice sight words used in the story.

1. Write each word listed on the right on two plain 3 x 5 inch cards, so you have two sets of cards. Using one set of cards, ask your child to repeat each word after you. Shuffle both decks of cards together, and deal three cards to each player. Put the remaining cards in a pile, face down.

2. Player 1 asks player 2 for a particular word. If player 2 has the word card, then he passes it to player 1. If player 2 does not have the word card, then he says, "Go fish," and player 1 takes a card from the pile. Player 2 takes a turn.

3. Whenever a player has two cards with the same word, he puts those cards down on the table and says the word out loud. The player with the most matches wins the game.

4. Keep the cards and combine them with other sight word cards you make. Use them all to play this game or play sight word games featured in other **We Read Phonics** books.

over

show

look

they

thumb

color

friend

crayon

behind

Magic tricks are fun to see.
And they are fun to do.

Try to do the tricks in this book.

This is what you will need.

Do the tricks over and over.
Do them until you get them
right. Then put on a show!

The first trick is "The Right Color."

A friend takes a crayon from a box.

You put your hands behind your back. He puts the crayon in your hand.

You do not look at it. But you
can tell your friends what color
it is! How do you do it?

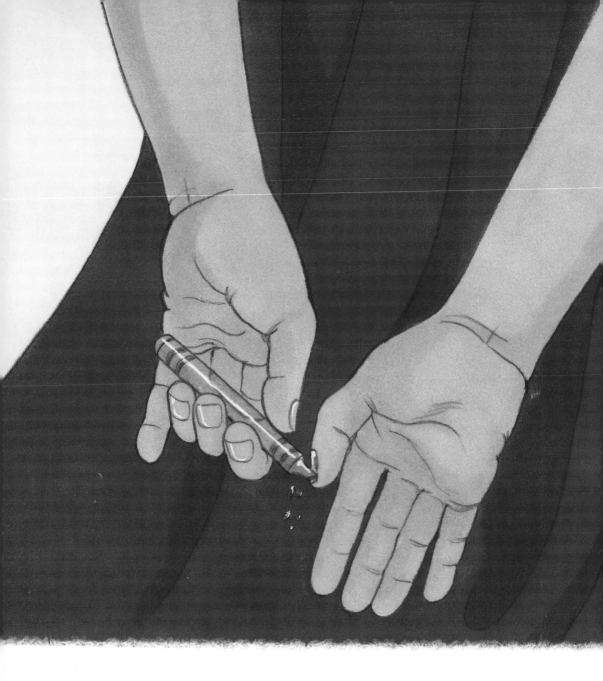

Scrape the crayon with your
nail. You should feel a bit of
the crayon under your nail.

Pretend you are thinking.

Look at the color on your nail.

Say, "The right color is ...." Then say
the name of the color on your nail.

Now show the crayon. Yes!
You have said the right color!

Now try this trick. This is
"The Clinging Pen."

Display a pen to your friends.
Do they see tape or glue? No!

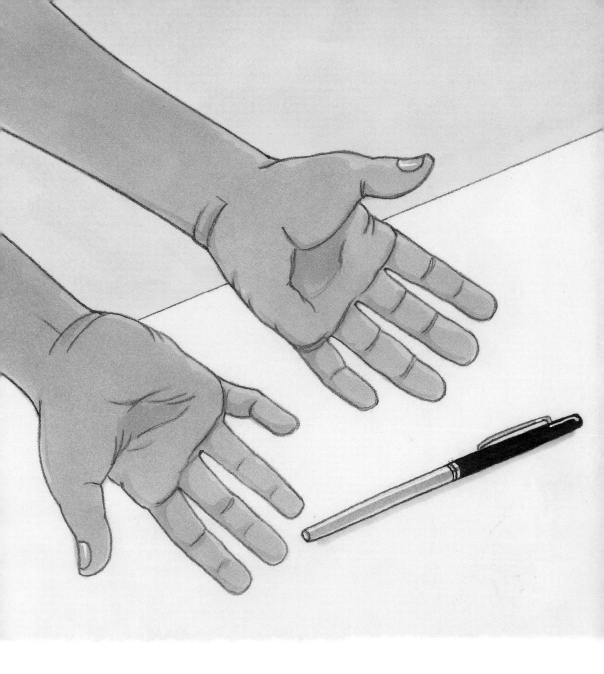

Display your hands. Do they
see tape or glue? No! Put the
pen in your left hand.

Grip the pen with your thumb. Then grip your left hand with your right hand. Do it like you see here.

Lift your left hand. Then lift you[r] thumb. The pen clings to your hand! How do you do it?

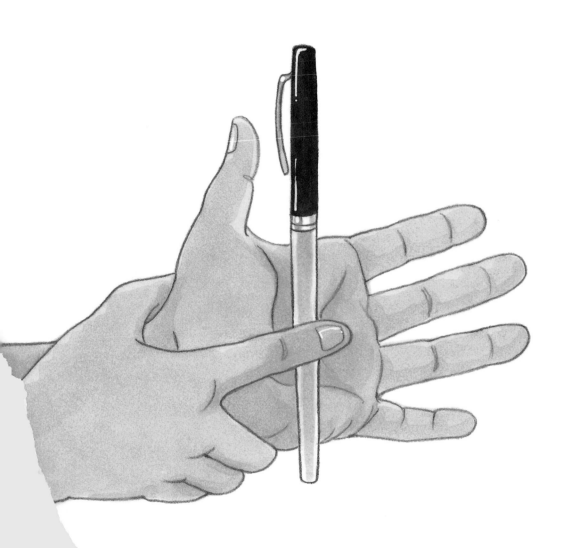

…s the index finger of your right
…nd. It keeps the pen in place!

These tricks are fun
and not too hard.

Put on a hat! Use a cape!

Have fun!

Word Search

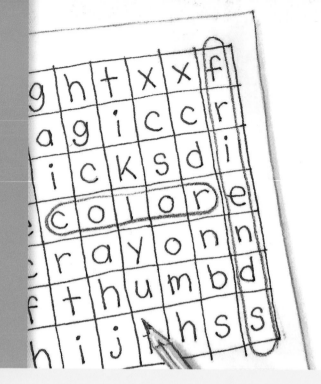

Rereading words from the story will help your child become more comfortable reading those words.

1 Make a grid on a sheet of paper (or use graph paper) that is 8 squares across and 7 down.

2 Write these letters on the first line, one letter per square:
r, i, g, h, t, x, x, f

3 Write these letters on the second line, one letter per square:
a, m, a, g, i, c, c, r

4 Write these letters on the third line, one letter per square:
t, r, i, c, k, s, d, i

5 Continue writing these letters on subsequent lines:
p, e, c, o, l, o, r, e
e, c, r, a, y, o, n, n
n, f, t, h, u, m, b, d
g, h, i, j, t, h, s, s

6 Now try to find these words in the word search. Words can be across or down. Circle the words when you find them.
right, magic, tricks, color, crayon, pen, friends, thumb

Word Families

This game will help your child read words that appear in this story, as well as words that have the same ending.

Materials: paper or cardboard; pencil, crayon or marker; and scissors

1. Make 6 cards that measure 2 x 3 inches. Print these six word family endings on the cards: **ail**, **ight**, **ame**, **ick**, **ie**, and **ay**.

2. Make 12 smaller letter cards that measure 2 x 2 inches. Print these letters on the cards: **f, l, m, n, p, r, s, t, c, d, b,** and **w**.

3. Place the larger word family cards face down in one pile. Place the smaller letter cards face down in a draw pile.

4. The players all take 3 cards from the pile of word family cards and place the cards face up in front of them. The first player then draws a card from the draw pile and tries to make a word using one of his word family endings. If a word can be made, the player places the card in front of the word ending. If a word cannot be made, the card is placed in a discard pile.

5. Play continues. Players can take a card from the draw pile or the discard pile. Players can make multiple words with each word family card, simply placing new letter cards on top of others.

6. Play ends when the draw pile is empty. The player who creates the most words wins. Mix the cards and play again!

If you liked *Magic Tricks,*
here is another **We Read Phonics** book you are sure to enjoy!

Talent Night

A young penguin is sure he will win the
talent contest. He does the most amazing
things! He has them laughing! He has them
gasping! No one could do better! No one,
that is, except maybe for shy little Pam.